A Practical Guide:
21 Days of Consecration

Monica L. Sanders, M.Div

ISBN: 9780988834552

Copyright ©2018 by Kingdom Living Publishing Company. All rights reserved. No part of this publication may be reproduced, stored in a retrieval system, or transmitted in any form or by any means, electronic, mechanical, photocopying, recording or otherwise, without the prior permission of the copyright owner.

Dedications

To my Kingdom Fellowship International Family
I love you and thank you for allowing me to be your Pastor.

To my Bishop, M. Neville Smith
Thank you for covering me and always offering Godly words and support. You are truly a Knight!

PREFACE

Dear Reader,

Use this as a guide to consecrating yourself before GOD. Read on each day. Reflect and write. Exercise. Eat healthy. And most of all pray, daily.

May you enjoy this journey as much, as I enjoyed preparing it for you. Let God be your guide and watch how you will be blessed.

Yours in HIS service,
Pastor Monica L. Sanders, M.Div.

Table of Contents
21 Days of Consecration

Day 1-Preparation
Day 2-Focus
Day 3-Prayer
Day 4-Affirmations
Day 5-Speak A Thang
Day 6-Relationships
Day 7-Giving
Day 8-Service to God and others
Day 9- Being A Constant and Consistent
Day 10-Stretching
Day11-Sabbath
Day 12-Forgiveness
Day 13-Honoring Men and Women of Faith
Day 14-Faithful
Day 15-The Truth
Day 16-Exercise
Day 17-Distractions
Day 18-Blessing in Disguise
Day 19-Sealed w/my Tears
Day 20-Make It Personal
Day 21-Selah & Reflect

1 Corinthians 6:19-20 Amplified Bible (AMP)

19 Do you not know that your body is a temple of the Holy Spirit who is within you, whom you have [received as a gift] from God, and that you are not your own [property]? 20 You were bought with a price [you were actually purchased with the precious blood of Jesus and made His own]. So then, honor and glorify God with your body.

Day 1 Preparation

Take time today to prepare your mind and body for consecration. Consecration is defined by vocabulary.com as "the act of dedicating something to God, sanctifying it and making it holy."

Ask yourself these questions:
1. What will you make holy for God in the next 21 days?
2. How will you sanctify yourself truly before God to make a difference in your life and the lives of others?

Take time to journal and pray.
Lord, allow this time of consecration to be an example of my love to you. May I dedicate myself to you in this moment and be mindful of your sacrifices for me. In Jesus' name, Amen.

_____

_____

_____

_____

_____

Day 2 Focus

As we continue our consecration, we will continue to prepare. Prepare to focus today. In the tech world there are software applications or Apps for short. Lifewire describes them as "It's a piece of software that can run through a web browser or even offline on your computer, phone, tablet or any other electronic device. Apps may or may not have a connection to the internet. The app is a modern take on the word software or application." I find if I have too many Apps open, especially on my mobile devices, my battery drains quickly (becomes weaker) in a matter of minutes. It may be at 100%, and when I look again, it's on 10%. If that is the case, I find myself scrambling to find the power cord to recharge or sometimes it just dies and takes several minutes to restore once connected. Our lives are this way. If we have too many things going on (Apps open) we drain very quickly. We scramble to find the power source to reconnect and sometimes we mentally or spiritually die. In the period of consecration, we must be able to focus on God even more and turn off unnecessary Apps. Apps can be anything that is draining you and distracting you.

Ask yourself these questions:
1. What is open in my life that is causing me to be de-replenished of God's Power?

2. How can I recharge to be able to stay connected to God, who is my Power source?

Take time to journal and pray.
Lord, allow me to focus and turn off the Apps in my life. Allow me to focus more on the plan you have for my day instead of planning it myself. Allow me to see what is truly important and concentrate on that alone. I'm turning off the Apps In Jesus' name, Amen.

_____

_____

_____

_____

_____

_____

_____

_____

_____

Day 3 Prayer

As we continue our consecration, we must begin to line up ourselves to pray effectively. What is prayer? The Blue Letter Bible defines prayer as "Prayer is talking to God. It is our way of communicating our thoughts, needs, and desires to Him." As we prepare; there must be a plan. Why a prayer agenda? As we prepare to speak with God, our prayer agenda is of the utmost importance. It gives details to our prayer and supplication to The Highest God. We wouldn't walk into an important meeting without preparing ourselves. Why do we go to an important meeting with God, without the same? Many times our prayers are not valid because one; we don't pray or pray fervently and two; we don't prepare to have the conversation with God so we cannot receive HIS will for our life. With that said, let's begin to formulate our prayer agenda.

Our prayer agenda should have the following:
1. **Reflection**-Reflect on how God has blessed you and your circumstances/situations. You want to be grateful but strategic.
2. **Write**-Write down your request for what it is you want to petition God for. Make sure you are a mature disciple in your request. Many times we go to God for things HE has already given us power and authority to do.

3. **Research**-Find and write out Scriptures concerning your request, they provide a framework for prayer. It allows you to pray accordingly.

Now, that you have formulated a plan for prayer, find that spot you meet God at and begin your conversation, however, make sure you take time for HIM to respond.

Thought to ponder:
Is my prayer agenda in The Will of God?

Take time to journal and pray.
Most Gracious God as I submit myself to you today, I offer my prayer agenda. John 14:14 says "If you ask Me anything in My name, I will do it." So, God, we ask these things in Jesus' name, Amen.

_____

_____

_____

_____

_____

_____

_____

Day 4 Affirmations

As we continue our consecration, let's talk affirmations. As you know once you set your mind to do something there are things that will discourage you and try to make you give up or give in. Therefore we need to equip ourselves with "emotional support and/or encouragement." My favorite affirmations come from Louise Hay. Louise was an incredible visionary and advocate. Everyone who had the privilege to meet her, either in person or through her words, felt her passion for serving others. Sadly, she passed away peacefully in her sleep, August 2017, at the age 90. Two of my favorite affirmations of hers is: "I am in the process of positive change." and "I am on an ever-changing journey." Of course, there are many more that motivate me, however those stand out.

During a time of consecration, it is key to focus on emotional support, especially as you fast (which we will deal with soon). Emotional support is essential as you begin to hear clearer and center yourself on the things of God for your journey.

Thought to ponder:
Louise Hay did an article entitled "What is Mirror Work?" She would say, "Mirror work is the most effective method I've found for learning to love yourself and see the world as a safe and loving place."

I encourage you through these days of consecration to focus on your Mirror Work. Begin to love yourself as God loves you. John 3:16 tells us "For God so loved the world that he gave his one and only Son, that whoever believes in him shall not perish but have eternal life." That's a lotta love going on!

1. Find affirmations that WILL encourage you. Don't wait on others to encourage, you must be your own cheerleader on this journey.
2. Post your affirmations, as a daily reminder.

Take time to journal and pray.
Dear God, we thank you for your love and your word that we can stand on. Help us to be encouraged each day. Provide us with what we need to deal with our emotions. Help us to focus on our work for you while you work on us. In Jesus' name, Amen.

_____

_____

_____

_____

_____

_____

Day 5 Speak A Thang

Consecration is easily spoken of however it's different when you decide to do it, especially in today's times. We are so busy with our lives that taking time to seek God for the greater is often put to the side or just a good thought. The time of consecration that you are seeking has to be spoken into existence so it can be done. I once preached a sermon called "Speak A Thing", from Proverbs 18:21 which states "Death and life are in the power of the tongue, and those who love it will eat its fruits." The sermon discussed how we could produce good and evil just by talking, which we do too much of at times. There is an idiom that says, "walk the walk and talk the talk." We seem to do the opposite we talk about doing. However, we don't do, and then God's work is left undone.

Going forward on this journey we must proclaim our tongue to match our mindset of Christ. We are a society that sabotages our own lives because we don't live or pray by the word. Deuteronomy 30:19, "I call heaven and earth to witness against you today that I have set before you life and death, blessings and curses. Choose life so that you and your descendants may live." Speak life and blessings as you face trials and tribulations. Understand that God is listening and waiting to fight your battles.

Scripture to Ponder:
Psalms 91:14-16

"Those who love me, I will deliver; I will protect those who know my name. When they call to me, I will answer them; I will be with them in trouble, I will rescue them and honor them. With long life I will satisfy them, and show them my salvation."

Time to journal and pray.
Lord, help me to, **Think** it into existence,
Pray it into existence, **Speak** it into existence,
Write it into existence, and **Work** it into existence.
In Jesus' Name, Amen.

_____

_____

_____

_____

_____

_____

_____

_____

_____

Day 6 Relationships

Relationships are a key factor during the consecration. Relationships can make you or break you. If you don't have the right people pouring into you, you could literally die. I often ponder that in many relationships, there is one-sidedness. There is a person that always gives and a person that takes. However, in a healthy relationship, there is a give and a take. Most sane people find themselves as givers while others take, constantly. It is important to have healthy relationships no matter your age or position in the relationship. A University of Washington Health study defined a Healthy relationship as "when two people develop a connection based on:
* Mutual respect
* Trust
* Honesty
* Support
* Fairness/equality
* Separate identities
* Good communication
* A sense of playfulness/fondness"

Healthy relationships includes being on one-accord especially in your faith.

Thoughts to ponder:
1. Are the important relationships in my life healthy? Why or why not?

2. Am I a person promoting the characteristics of a healthy relationship based on the connection outlined above?

Time to journal and pray.

God, Thank you for all those who promote a healthy relationship in my life and please help me to reciprocate. Help me to identify the healthy relationship that lines up in my faith and love towards you. In Jesus' Name, Amen.

_____

_____

_____

_____

_____

_____

_____

_____

Day 7-Giving

The most significant story of giving is Jesus dying on the Cross for our sins (1 Peter 2:24). God placed himself in a human named Jesus to die for our sins and give us salvation. What a gift to offer, the gift of love and the gift of salvation. Giving is a big part of our love towards Christ and we should be thankful for all that GOD has done for our lives. However, we have difficulty in giving. Giving of our time, our talent and of course our money. Yet, it never belonged to us anyway.

I love the way The Message Bible explains it in Malachi 3:8-11, " Begin by being honest. Do honest people rob God? But you rob me day after day. "You ask, 'How have we robbed you?' The tithe and the offering—that's how! And now you're under a curse—the whole lot of you—because you're robbing me. Bring your full tithe to the Temple treasury so there will be ample provisions in my Temple. Test me in this and see if I don't open up heaven itself to you and pour out blessings beyond your wildest dreams. For my part, I will defend you against marauders, protect your wheat fields and vegetable gardens against plunderers." The Message of God-of-the-Angel-Armies."

Giving is unique and has its rewards. Does God need your money? No, however, it is your duty unto him according to HIS Word. The great thing about giving, its benefits are blessings, "pour out blessings beyond your wildest dreams" is what is promised. How beautiful to know that your investment will yield blessings beyond what you can think or imagine. We always think about the benefits of money, but how about the blessings of health, peace, healthy relationship, and faith.

Thoughts to Ponder:
1. How is my giving?
2. Should I be giving more unto The Lord?
3. Am I a constant tither?

Time to journal and pray.
Amazing GOD, you have provided so much for me, and I am grateful. Help me to provide what I need for you especially in my giving. Help me to sow seeds on fertile grown and be a blessing. Show me how to be a blessing to The Kingdom of God and those who you choose for me to bless. I thank you. In Jesus' name, Amen.

_____

_____

_____

_____

Day 8 Service to God and others

What are you doing for others?

As we celebrate Dr. King this day, remember he was one who left us a legacy of service. The idea of service can be explained biblically in Galatians 5:13-14 "For you were called to freedom, brothers, and sisters; only do not use your freedom as an opportunity for self-indulgence, but through love become slaves to one another. For the whole law is summed up in a single commandment, "You shall love your neighbor as yourself." A life of service is a sacrifice many have accomplished for our wellbeing. Many like Dr. King who we are celebrating as I write on this day. The National Constitutional Center explains, "Dr. Martin Luther King Jr. saw himself as a servant of humanity, and he wanted his life to be remembered as a life of service to others." We must draw our inspiration from Dr. King and discern how we can serve God and others.

Questions to Ponder:
1. Do you participate in acts of service for others?
2. Name some ways that you have or can get involved in acts of service?

Time to journal and pray.
God, thank you for all those who have served like Jesus to make this world a better place. Thank you for sacrifice

and labor in service. Help me be as committed to serve and walk in purpose. In Jesus' name, Amen.

Day 9 Being A Constant and Consistent

You are on Day 9, and I am sure you are feeling a little weary. I know you are being attacked and annoyed by life's little distractions. Today's word is on Being A Constant and Consistent. I love the definitions by Dictionary.com. It defines Constant as "1. not changing or varying" "2. continuing without pause or letup; unceasing:" Consistent mean "constantly adhering to the same principles," These words are so often interchangeable. However, have we been both in Christ?

To help with this process, think about the Polaris or as we know it, the North Star. The North Star appears consistent in the sky because, it is said to be positioned closest to the line of the axis of The Earth into space. It has been proven the only bright star whose position is relative to a rotating Earth, and it does not change. All other stars appear to move opposite to the Earth's rotation. It stays stationary like Jesus. Hebrews 13:8 tells us, "Jesus Christ is the same yesterday and today and forever." Jesus is and has been a constant; he's been consistent! It is a relief in a changing world that we can identify a constant and something is consistent.

Ponder on this:
1. How have we been a constant/consistent in God?
2. What can we do to begin/continue this process?

Take time to journal and pray.

Lord, help me to not be all over the place. Help me to hear you say. "Well done, thou good and faithful servant: thou hast been faithful over a few things, I will make thee ruler over many things: enter thou into the joy of thy lord." (Matthew 25:21) In Jesus' name, Amen.

_____

_____

_____

_____

_____

_____

_____

_____

_____

_____

_____

Day 10-Stretching

Do you feel the stretch of consecration? As we labor through days of consecration, you should begin to fill the stretching of your mind, body, and spiritual soul. You should be becoming more attentive, more annoyed and more determined.
1. More attentive to the focus of God.
2. More annoyed with pettiness and #fakenews.
3. More determined to continue and hear God's instructions.

Stretching does for the spirit what it does for the body. The benefits of stretching are, "The body relies on being stretched, much like a car needs regularly servicing. ... Improves circulation – Stretching increases the blood flow to your muscles, thus improving your circulation. Relieves stress – Stretching relaxes tense muscles that often accompany stress. This helps relax the mind as well."

Just like the body relies on being stretched so does your mind and spirit. It needs the servicing to improve your thought pattern to increase the mindset of a mature disciple. We have mortal being needs to relieve stress and tension. However, we need to pray and release our thoughts, anxieties, and fears to The Lord. Many of us as Christians walk around stressed and never take time to stretch out in GOD. God has always provided and been there; however, we are looking for physical being instead of relying on God. Stretching helps you to achieve better form and flexibility. The stretch is to lean and depend on God no matter what.

Prevention.com tells us of 7 Incredible Results You Can Get From Stretching Every day and I want to you consider them spiritually as well as physically.

1. You'll be bright-eyed and raring to go—even at 3 PM. (I Peter 5:8) New King James Version (NKJV), "Be sober, be vigilant; because your adversary the devil walks about like a roaring lion, seeking whom he may devour."

2. You will be less likely to trip and fall. (Jude 24-25) King James Version (KJV), "Now unto him that is able to keep you from falling, and to present you faultless before the presence of his glory with exceeding joy, To the only wise God our Saviour, be glory and majesty, dominion and power, both now and ever. Amen."

3. You'll move around more easily and with less pain. But I will restore you to health and heal your wounds,' declares the LORD" ~ (Jeremiah 30:17)

4. You'll make the most of your sweat session. (Psalm 66:10-12 ESV), "For you, O God, have tested us; you have tried us as silver is tried. You brought us into the net; you laid a crushing burden on our backs;

you let men ride over our heads; we went through fire and   through water; yet you have brought us out to a place of abundance."

5. You might be less likely to injure yourself. (Luke 21:36 ESV), "But stay awake at all times, praying that you may have strength to escape all these things that are going to take place, and to stand before the Son of Man."

6. You may lower your blood sugar. (Jeremiah 33:6 ESV), "Behold, I will bring to it health and healing, and I will heal them and reveal to them abundance of prosperity and security."

7. You'll stress less. Matthew 6:25-28 (NIV), "Therefore I tell you, do not worry about your life, what you will eat or drink; or about your body, what you will wear. Is not life more than food, and the body more than clothes? Look at the birds of the air; they do not sow or reap or store away in barns, and yet your heavenly Father feeds them. Are you not much more valuable than they? Can anyone of you by worrying add a single hour to your life? And why do you worry about clothes? See how the flowers of the field grow. They do not labor or spin."

Take the stretching results and turn them into spiritual principles and be calm and watch God work. Let's stretch today and move forward with God like never before.

Time to journal and pray.
God, my heart, and mind are open to stretching today. I know you will not give any more than I can handle. We love you and thank you for your patience with us. We know that your WILL shall be done in my life. In Jesus' Name I pray, Amen.

_____

_____

_____

_____

_____

_____

_____

_____

Day 11-Sabbath

(Exodus 20:8-11 ESV) "Remember the Sabbath day, to keep it holy. Six days you shall labor, and do all your work, but the seventh day is a Sabbath to the Lord your God. On it you shall not do any work, you, or your son, or your daughter, your male servant, or your female servant, or your livestock, or the sojourner who is within your gates. For in six days the Lord made heaven and earth, the sea, and all that is in them, and rested on the seventh day. Therefore the Lord blessed the Sabbath day and made it holy."

Let's talk today about Sabbath, Yes Sabbath. Do you have a day and time for Sabbath? I attended a conference in 2015 in Salisbury, North Carolina with Dr. Matthew Sleeth. Dr. Sleeth re-introduced me to "Remember the Sabbath." He begins to speak on how we must provide a "life-giving prescription for healthier and more God-centered life." God's commandment was to remember the Sabbath because he knew we would forget. Often we do forget about the Sabbath let alone keeping it holy. I believe we think rest will happen with our busy and chaotic lives. We believe we are invisible and maybe we don't need to set aside time. Defining the Sabbath is to find the day that you can keep holy, being realistic and actually doing it. Dr. Sleeteeh book entitled, 24/6: A Prescription for a healthier, happier life, tells us "rest doesn't just happen, It takes intentionality, commitment, and restraint.

Yet the rewards are indescribably amazing." Know that rest is important to you not only physically but mentally and spiritually as well.

Thoughts to Ponder:
1. What is Rest to you?
2. Do you have a day and time of Sabbath? If so, are you committed to it?

Time to journal and pray.
Pray this Poem:

      A Sabbath Poem by John David Walt:
                  Breathe
              rest in Rest,
            holy Leisure—
            airtight Time:
              Sabbath.
            hearing Ears,
          Creation slowing—
             open Eyes:
              Sabbath.
          guiltless Feasting,
          sacred Rhythms—
          Heaven Hugging:
              Sabbath.
          Nothing-doing
          Nowhere-going—
          Work unknowing:
              Sabbath.

Day 12-Forgiveness

We remember on a Forgiveness Friday, what Jesus did on the Cross, to forgive us for our sins. Forgiveness is becoming a forbidden subject. We stubbornly hold unforgiveness in our heart, as if it was our heartbeat. Wonder if Jesus did not die for our sins, we would be in an unforgiven state with God. In this time of consecration, we must forgive and forget, however we will have wisdom in taking up relationships, tasks and or assignment as it relates to our forgiveness.

(Mark 11:25 Amplified Bible AMP) tells us,
"Whenever you stand praying, if you have anything against anyone, forgive him [drop the issue, let it go], so that your Father who is in heaven will also forgive you your transgressions and wrongdoings [against Him and others]." The key to this scripture is "to drop the issue, let it go"! I have come to realize in my time on this earth, if you hold on to unforgiveness, that person, place or thing hold you hostage, and you will never be able to live freely in Christ. That "thing" will always lurk in the background trying to pull you back in a state of unforgiveness.

Mediate on this scripture:
(Matthew 18: 21) Then Peter came to Jesus and asked, "Lord, how many times shall I forgive my brother who sins against me? Up to seven times?"

Time to journal and pray.
God, thank you for giving us Jesus to forgive us for our sins. Help me to forgive as you forgave us. Help me to not bare burdens from the past, but to walk in the present to prepare for my future. Help me to "drop the issue, let it go." In Jesus' name, Amen.

_____

_____

_____

_____

_____

_____

_____

_____

_____

_____

Day 13-Honoring Men and Women of Faith

Without integrity and honor. Having everything means nothing. -Robin Sharma.

We "stand on the shoulders" of so many great people, and we should feel blessed. Many, who turned little into much, because they were visionaries. Many, who sacrificed their lives to introduce us to a better tomorrow. Visionaries are those who could see the future and wanted it. Many today are so bogged down with the past, that their future is an after-thought. We don't take the time to honor men and women of faith anymore. I'm not talking about your Pastor, organizational leather or even your favorite preacher. I'm speaking of those men and women
1. Who prayed for you?
2. Who sowed into your life?
3. Who told you right from wrong even when you did not ask for their advice?

We forget those who paved the way, and it allows for not only complacency to set in, but entitlement.

I purchased a shirt that said, "I am my ancestors wildest dreams." I'm wondering if that is positive or negative. Free Dictionary.com defines wildest dreams as "All the things that one has ever imagined or hoped."

However, we are our ancestor's nightmare. Nightmares, when we do not walk in purpose, respect who we are and who we can become. Proverbs 10:9, tells us "Whoever walks in integrity walks securely, but he who makes his ways crooked will be found out." We are obligated to walk with integrity and honor those who have come before us. It is out of respect and glory for the cloud of witnesses.

Scripture to ponder:
Hebrews 12:1, "Therefore, since we are surrounded by such a great cloud of witnesses, let us throw off everything that hinders and the sin that so easily entangles. And let us run with perseverance the race marked out for us," What does this mean to you?
Name your cloud of witnesses.

Time to journal and pray.
Most gracious God, Help me to honor you and the men and women that you allowed to walk in their purpose for me to have a purpose. I am grateful for my life and your favor. Continue to lead and guide me with your clear instructions. In Jesus' Name, Amen.

_____

_____

_____

_____

Day 14-Faithful

(Hebrews 11:1 King James Version KJV) "Now faith is the substance of things hoped for, the evidence of things not seen."

Faith is something that we say we have however, let's make sure we do. Many things try our patience and also may delay us, as we are on this journey to fulfill our purpose. Our faith has to be strong to endure the distractions and aggravations of life. Our hope as a Child of the Highest God is to be strong, determined and committed. Dr. Martin Luther King, Jr. once said, "Faith is taking the first step even when you don't see the whole staircase." As Christians our first step to faith was to accept Jesus as our Lord and Savior and to understand the benefits of being a child of God. Knowing this does not mean we don't go through or have problems. What it means is, because of our faith, we will get through it, and all of our questions, will be handled by God as we walk in our faith. We must step in faith, and the world of God as trials and tribulations come, our faith has to become big along with our Spirit. Once that happens, the faith walk happens. We must surround ourselves with the Word of God; it shall become our light. Psalm 119:105 tell us his Word becomes a lamp until our feet.

Questions to Ponder:
1. On a scale of 1-5 (5 the highest) where is your faith walk?

2. Are you consistent in having faith that GOD will and can?
3. Do you need to strengthen your faith?

Time to journal and pray.
Most heavenly God, Thank you for always showing us your belief in us, however I need you now to teach me how to have strong faith, renewed faith and/or everlasting faith in you. I do trust and believe in you, make me consistent and help me to endure. In Jesus' Name, Amen.

_____

_____

_____

_____

_____

_____

_____

_____

Day 15-The Truth

As we figure out this world and The Word, we must know the Truth.

I think this is a struggle today, figuring out what is true. We now have what is called Fake News. Merriam-Webster defines Fake News as "Fake news is frequently used to describe a political story which is seen as damaging to an agency, entity, or person." In other words it's a lie to defraud. Which would be found as the opposite of truth in our eyes. Scripture is clearly stated in John 8:32 ESV, "And you will know the truth, and the truth will set you free." Clearly speaking if we know the truth we are unconfined in your walk, thoughts and talk. You can pursue a gentle more pure examination of the world and all those who are around you. The truth offers a prescription for honesty and integrity that is inviting.

2 Timothy 2:15 tell you to "Do your best to present yourself to God as one approved, a worker who does not need to be ashamed, rightly handling the word of truth." The truth is an essential piece of honoring God and being his servant-leader. I once heard T.D. Jakes say that a leader does not talk about the problem, they talk about how to solve the problem. Truth knows what is right from wrong. In essence, truth provides clarity ethically not only to our lives but our purpose.

Questions to ponder:
1. What is your definition of truth?
2. Does it align with the true definition of what truth is?

Time to journal and pray.
God, we offer ourselves to you.
Help us to live a John 4:24 life understanding, You are the spirit, and if I worship you, I must worship you in spirit and truth. In Jesus' Name, Amen.

_____

_____

_____

_____

_____

_____

_____

_____

_____

Day 16-Exercise

Endure...you are at Day 16...give yourself a hand. Now its time to exercise, you are mentally strong now let's get physically strong and healthy.

As we move forward today, it is time to exercise your body. Yes, exercise! 3 John 1:2 ESV tells us, "Beloved, I pray that all may go well with you and that you may be in good health, as it goes well with your soul." We have spent time dealing with our minds and our spirit, which we are not finished however, exercise is essential to our consecration as well. Believe me, it is not a favorite topic of mind, and I am not enthusiastic about it either. However, it is essential therefore we must take the time to exercise at your appropriate level. You must figure out what works for you and do it. If you have a medical condition, please consult your physician first. Even ask your physician for directions. He or She may recommend a healthy diet, exercise plan and one of my favorites, water aerobics. Remember 1 Corinthians 6:19 says, "Don't you know that your body is the temple of the Holy Spirit, who lives in you and who was given to you by God? You do not belong to yourselves but to God."

WebMD.com tells us "Your heart, your brain – your entire body – benefits from exercise and exercise becomes even more important as you get older. You naturally lose muscle mass with age, which slows down your metabolism." So the benefit of exercise is a plus, not only for your body, but your heart and your brain.

Ponder these questions?
1. What will be the first thing you do towards your physical fitness?
2. What is stopping you from getting started?

Time to journal and pray.
Lord, help me to live 1 Corinthians 9:27 ESV
"But I discipline my body and keep it under control," Help me not to talk the talk but to walk the walk as it relates to my body. Help me to be healthy so that I can continue to do your work. Help me to set a plan and be determined to stick to it. In Jesus' Name, Amen.

_____

_____

_____

_____

_____

Day 17-Distractions

As I even write this, the adversary is trying his best to distract me. Let's be sure of how we define distraction. Google defines it as "a thing that prevents someone from giving full attention to something else." However, I define a distraction as something that plays on your emotions and is there to agitate you, like a fly at a barbecue, to frustrate you and get you out of focus.

Distractions allow your attention to be turned to something that most of the time is irrelevant to your purpose. Don't be fooled by the mundane things that the devil throws at you. You must recognize the signs.

1. Something or someone comes out of nowhere and attacks you;
2. You cannot focus on what God has placed before you; and
3. You make excuses. Distractions are temptations for you to be stalled in your purpose. Stay focus and understand that you are almost there, don't be distracted.

Scripture to Ponder:
1 Corinthians 10:13 ESV
"No temptation has overtaken you that is not common to man. God is faithful, and he will not let you be tempted beyond your ability, but with the temptation he will also provide the way of escape, that you may be able to endure it."

Time to journal and pray.
Psalm 19:14,
"Let the words of my mouth and the meditation of my heart be acceptable in your sight, O Lord, my rock and my redeemer." Help me to stay faithful, focus and on fire for you. In Jesus Name, Amen.

_____

_____

_____

_____

_____

_____

_____

_____

_____

_____

Day 18-Blessing in Disguise

As we have been praying and fasting and hopefully journaling during this consecration period, we have also been blessed. However, we must remind ourselves that blessings don't always come in a way we imagine however they do occur.

1. A blessing of unexpected finances
2. A blessing of an assignment to show appreciation
3. A blessing of a relaxing evening doing nothing
4. A blessing of a phone call to an answered prayer for health and well-being

The blessings that you pray for will come, however, you continue your journey as God works. This is called a blessing in disguise. We know God is able and capable however it is wrapped up in surprise.

"Blessings can be associated with protection and happiness. God's blessings protects us, and help to guide us to the path of happiness and righteousness. Use these Bible verses to remind you of the ultimate blessing of protection promised to us, when Jesus died for us on the cross, and use them as a direction to the right path He intended for us." (BibleStudytools.com)

So, the next time you receive an unexpected blessing, remember to first thank God for your blessing(s) in disguise.

Scriptures to Ponder:

Philippians 4:19 NIV, "And my God will meet all your needs according to the riches of his glory in Christ Jesus."

and

James 1:17 NIV, " Every good and perfect gift is from above, coming down from the Father of the heavenly lights, who does not change like shifting shadows."

Time to journal and pray.

God, I thank you for your blessings in disguise. Please help me to remember my prayers, but most of all are grateful for my blessings. In Jesus' Name, Amen.

_____

_____

_____

_____

_____

_____

Day 19 Sealed w/my Tears

As we soar through life it is important to keep track.

I have journaled my thoughts to God for years. My youngest daughter and others have become journalers because of my testament of how it helps and heals. Journaling has caused me inspiration, release and of course reflection. I have journaled about my hurts, disappointments and of course my victories. The reflection moments in our lives need to be recorded for reminders and celebration that we may forget. I remember organizing and found older journals and I began to read through them. One journal was of troubling times. I began to reflect on how I would journal and cry. Years later, rereading what I have written, some of the pages were stuck together. I wondered what happened, why are these pages stuck and God reminded me, 'I sealed it with your tears.' Psalm 56:8-9The Message (MSG) tells us, "You've kept track of my every toss and turn through the sleepless nights, each tear entered in your ledger, each ache written in your book. If my enemies run away, turn tail when I yell at them, Then I'll know that God is on my side." Many things we go through after God has healed us, God seals. I was and I am still grateful for this one reminder from God for my healing through my journaling. My journaling also reminded me that God was right there healing me through something as small as my writing, even when I didn't realize it. Many times, we go through and God is there, watching us carefully.

Action:
1. Begin or continue to journal!
2. If you have been journaling, take time to reflect with your journals.

Time to journal and pray.

Thank you, God for sealing my tears and bringing healing through my journaling, my paper conversation with you. Help me to take a moment out of each day to write out my prayers, my thoughts, and your wisdom. In Jesus' Name, Amen.

_____

_____

_____

_____

_____

_____

_____

_____

Day 20-Make It Personal

We are almost there, stay focused. We are in the last stretch of our concentration.

Do you have a personal statement? Normally personal statements are "a written description of one's achievements, interests, etc., included as part of an application for a job or to an educational program." However, I would like for you to really make it personal. I would like for you to write how you will continue on this spiritual journey. Discuss what measures you will take to receive your goals. The scripture below outlines the importance of writing your vision.

Ponder this scripture:
Habakkuk 2:1-3 King James Version (KJV)
" I will stand upon my watch, and set me upon the tower, and will watch to see what he will say unto me, and what I shall answer when I am reproved. And the Lord answered me, and said, Write the vision, and make it plain upon tables, that he may run that readeth it. For the vision is yet for an appointed time, but at the end it shall speak, and not lie: though it tarry, wait for it; because it will surely come, it will not tarry."

Final Thought:

Many times we take too long to understand the importance of our journey. Each day is a gift and we must be not only guided, but reminded. If we write out and become personal with it, we will be determined to accomplish what we set out to do.

Action:
1. Write your personal statement;
2. Frame it; and
3. Place it somewhere you can see it each day.

Time to journal and pray.

Lord, help me to write the vision and make it plain. Give me your thoughts and actions for my life. In Jesus' name, Amen.

_____

_____

_____

_____

_____

_____

_____

Day 21-Selah & Reflect

Reflection-"a fixing of the thoughts on something; careful consideration."

Wow, we have reached Day 21!

You have spent the past 20 days on focusing, praying and prayerful practical teaching on self-improvement. The past 20 days were about committing and strengthening ourselves for resolutions for healthy living. Romans 12:2 (ESV) "Do not be conformed to this world, but be transformed by the renewal of your mind, that by testing you may discern what is the will of God, what is good and acceptable and perfect." The challenge for today is to discern and reflect on what went wrong and what improved during your days of consecration.

As we reflect we want to make sure this experience was not a ritual, however, a resolution, working hard towards making yourself better. Many times we make short-term goals that become rituals, however we pray that you reflect on how you can make evolutions out of what has transpired during this time of consecration.

Questions to Ponder:
1. What transpired within you during the past 21 days?
2. What will you do further to stay focus?
3. How will you be practical going forward?

Scripture:
Proverbs 16:3 (ESV)
"Commit your work to the Lord, and your plans will be established."

Time to journal and pray.
God, thank you for your days of consecration. Thank you for allowing me to stay focus on the areas that I need development. Please let me continue to commit myself to you so your plans for my life can be established and I may be stronger and a witness to your love and care. In Jesus' Name, Amen and Amen.

Many reflect in devotion at certain times of the year. However, we hope that you take time to consecrate yourself, often especially in this chaotic world.

Thank you for taking this 21 days of focus.
We pray you were encouraged and discovered your true self. May your days be of healthy relationships and kindness to yourself and most of all commitment to Our Lord and Savior, Jesus The Christ.

www.ingramcontent.com/pod-product-compliance
Lightning Source LLC
Chambersburg PA
CBHW081328190426
43193CB00044B/2889